Breakfast in Memphis

Vol. 2
Midnight in the Desert

Mark Randall Mueller

Cover Art by Analy Nakat

ISBN: 979-8-9885322-4-8
EBOOK: 979-8-9885322-1-7
Library of Congress: 9798988532248
Cover Art by Analy Nakat
Instagram: @analynakat
www.analynakat.com

Breakfast in Memphis: Midnight in the Desert

Dedicated to the evolving education of mankind and the great revealing of truth in the best interest of us all.

Breakfast in Memphis: Midnight in the Desert

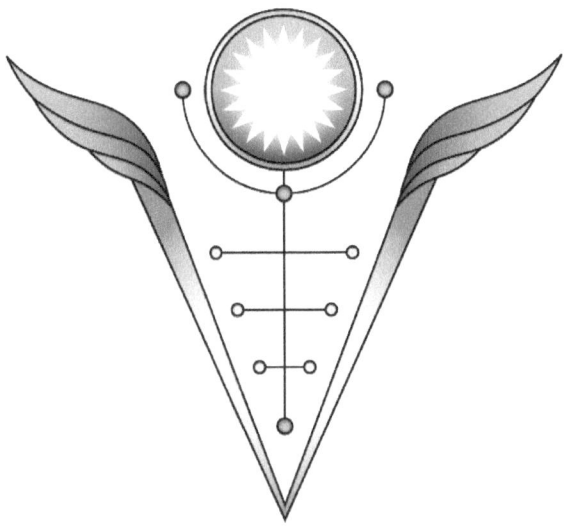

Truth and Justice League was founded from the realization that we live in an unjust and badly contaminated world and that without a positive vision for the future and the participation of ordinary people, destruction of the human species is inevitable. In the summer of 2019 we hosted a special event called the What if? Party to connect with and inspire a community of scientists, doctors, lawyers, journalists, filmmakers, environmental and social justice activists, churches, regenerative agriculturalists, artists, musicians, educators, healers, and many others to combine in their own unique ways to create a more sustainable, equitable and peaceful world.

Cont'd...

Breakfast in Memphis: Midnight in the Desert

Do well by doing good. It is important to remember we are here to live free, pursue happiness and avoid hurting others through violence, carelessness, greed, toxic exposure, fraudulent business practices, discrimination, prejudice or hate.

Truth and Justice League's mission is to assist in the creative evolution of the legal system to improve the balance of fairness and justice in the lives of all people. Join us in becoming part of the solution. Let's build a better future, together we rise!

FOREWORD

Breakfast in Memphis Vol. 2: Midnight in the Desert is a collection of poems reflecting on the current chaotic, divisive, and toxic condition of mankind, America, and the planet. I hope the poems will be thought-provoking, lead to greater awareness of the patterns and root causes which have led to the "code red" for humanity, so that we can work together for solutions for the betterment of all.

Breakfast in Memphis: Midnight in the Desert

What if?
We bypassed the fear
And ignored the confusion
And do what we can do now
Without worrying about
The rest of it
Or what others have done
Or will do
And without giving any power at
All to those known or unknown
Who seek to block us, diffuse us
Defeat us or mislead us,
What if?
We started this today?
No ego, no shame, no regrets
No winners or losers
Or too small or too old
This is a co-ed team
Whatever that means in
This day and age

Gender, race, politics, religion
Educational degrees, resumes and achievements, past trauma
Past lives, personal history
Family problems, bank accounts,
Debts and credits
Leave them in the locker room
They just weigh us down
And divide us
If you need a uniform one will be provided
You pick your own number, symbol or name

Cont'd…

Who wants to play?

The field is open
I've got a ball

Keep it simple
Have fun
Like when we were kids
Imaginary is real
We have energy
And health
We are young and strong
There are no limits
Who wants in?
Say when

Aho

Wizard Bear Speaks
Breakfast in Memphis

Warning 18+

This collection of poems contains adult topics, explicit language,
raw emotional content, imaginary worlds, and harsh examination
of self and others including many political/religious/corporate and
government agencies.

November Rains

November rains
Came calling
On Sunday afternoon
Cold cleansing showers
Falling on my head
Tear drops from heaven
Upon our dirty age
Can it wash away
Some evil or perhaps
The guilt and blame
November rain kept falling
But the world still looks
The same

Costumes

As I age
Not always
So gracefully
I am learning
To appreciate
The beauty of masks
And what they
Are revealing
And concealing
In the midst
Of this masquerade
We know as "life"

Breakfast in Memphis: Midnight in the Desert

God of Time

Every other Monday
And most days in between
I wake up maskless,
Naked and alone
Wearing socks in the summer
And wondering why
Fear is a weapon
I point at myself
My shield
Of confidence
Humor and grace
Got lost in the darkness
Or just ran away
Trust your gut
Your body knows
They all say
My gut wants to hide
A shivering chihuahua
The God of time
Tells me I have to get up
My guts loud and clear
A cigarette
Coffee
Whisky
Adderall
And blow
One out of 5
Will have to do
God of time
Says you gotta get up

Breakfast in Memphis: Midnight in the Desert

Digital Wine

Facebook/TikTok
Pornhub, Only Fans
Cam girls and trannies
All at Xhamster
Blue screen Viagra
Electronic blow
Digital wine
How relaxing
Cabernet
Malbec
Champagne
Merlot
Digital money
Credit card
Payments
Easy to promise
Harder to pay
Electronic vampires
Emptying pockets
Mortgaging lives
Sucking down energy
Motivation and pride
And showing you
How to suck your own dicks
While you stay locked inside

Clip and Chip

Clip and chip
Clip and chip
Off to war we go
Clip and chip
Clip and chip
Plastic in blood
Are we human at all
Clip and chip
Clip and chip
We are killing you
Now trust us to
Fix it
Clip and chip
Clip and chip
I can't seem to
Get it
Trained to sit
Stay and roll over
All for a treat
Clip and chip

Chip and clip
Devices to teach us
And guide us
Soon big brother
We promise
We will
Get it right
Clip and chip
Clip and chip
Electronic treats
Electronic punishment
Clip and chip
Clip and chip
Good little toy soldiers
Till the day that we die
Ya mon
Good little toy soldiers
Till the day that we die
Clip and chip
Clip and chip
Ya mon

Breakfast in Memphis: Midnight in the Desert

Lists and Notes

Lists and notes
Written down
And soon forgotten
Accomplishing nothing
But the ink
On the paper
Do we think
We will do them later?
Transfer of the assignment
From the nagging gut
And
Mind to the
Clean and innocent paper
All too often left
Undone, untouched and just
Forgotten
And so the dreams
Are left abandoned
Yet always wanting to
Be allowed to play
From the fields of our imagination

To our lives from day to day
Liberate those dreams from paper
The white or yellow faded graves
Are not the way to die

Carry on…try harder

Suppression of the Goddess

Block block
Access denied
The dagger of anger
Cuts deep inside
Throat choked
Gagged and tied
Memories repeat
They will not die
Arise and try
Again
Pretty please
This time maybe
Sorry lady
Next time maybe
Not yet woman
Can't you see
We change the rules
Just for you
Each time
Block block
Access denied
Block block
Choked and tied
Give up bitch
At least you tried
Go home woman
Why don't you cry?

Breakfast in Memphis: Midnight in the Desert

Divine Pesticide

Thank you Dow
For breakfast
Farben/Monsanto/Bayer provided lunch
Dinner was all you Wall Street
Thank you, DuPont, for
The poison pans to
Cook those toxic stews
Thank you industrial and war machines
For delicious chemicals
Straight up recognition
To the Nazis, CIA and you
Paperclip me Jesus
Nature never this easy
We didn't have the time

The End

Shut the door
Turn off the lights
I don't want to do it anymore

Johnny Midnight

2 A.M.
Forever midnight

What can be done
To break this spell

Forever midnight
Lost in time

Forever midnight
What is my name

Forever midnight
This is insane

Breakfast in Memphis: Midnight in the Desert

Heavenly Dilemmas
(Another Form of Hell)

Not now Mother Mary
Can't you see
I'm busy
No time
For playing
Kids
Keep acting
Crazy...
Jesus moved
To Vegas
At least he's got
A job
Satan betting heavy
Odds against human
Survival now @100-1
How could I have been so wrong
A miracle of creation
And only 6 days to market
By Sunday chilling out
Lucifer the Lawyer asking questions
Now...
Where is
Your testing?
Looks like a
Design defect
Rushed to market
Better call the Vatican
Tell 'em up those cash reserves
Lucifer lawyer and Charlie McDragon MD/JD
Devil & Dragon law firm

Cont'd...

Hard to beat in court
Filed the case last week
Playing for blood
The papers said
Changing the rules of the game
Vatican fired the bishops, bookies
They always got it wrong
But God was on their side?
Placing bets on altar boys/priests?
A parlor game from hell
Always the
Home court advantage
And nuns were keeping score
There is no first mistake
For clergy on the prowl
That mistake was being born
These all boy schools just made it worse
I shoulda known better
Look what they did to Eden
Monsanto, Dupont, Exxon?
No one cleans it up,
Spoiled trust fund fucks
It's time to cut you off
"Thoughts and prayers?"
How'd that work with Covid
When people don't prepare
Santa Claus gets thoughts and prayers
He calls it Christmas wishes
Adios

Breakfast in Memphis: Midnight in the Desert

Dirty Rain

Dirty rain
Austin, Texas
Little Los Angeles
Heading toward Bangladesh
God's tears
Tremendous regret

Street Dogs and Sunshine

Street dogs and sunshine
Masks and parades
Little ram was a ship's captain
Zebra first mate
Charlie and Frank built the boat
Life in Mexico is pulling me in
Waves in the darkness
One more perfect day
They call it paradise
I have to agree

Cathedral of Hope

Cathedral of Hope
Architect of dreams
Magnificent ruins
What happens to us
In the great
In-between?
Octopus of desire
Turning to greed
Stumbling quite slowly
Then
Crumbling fast
Swirls of patterns
Blueprints of design
Fingerprints of madness
In exquisite design
Musical physics
Frequency and waves
Harmony…ecstasy
Peace, love, and magic
A hovering perfection just
Out
Of reach?
A little more love
And some

Golden line intentions

Waiting to receive
Divine interventions
Galactic guidance
Says just hold on
We can make it
It is written
It is so
Yellow brick highways
Curve in the sky

Cont'd…

Breakfast in Memphis: Midnight in the Desert

Green
Emerald cities
In shimmering relief
We must be in Oz
Or somewhere near Phoenix
Babycakes whispered to her
Sisters…pink Cherry and green Creamie
Not yet said Uni
Unicorn Park is in Kansas

Griffins and crows
Are guarding the gold
Pyramids...mountains
Stories retold
Vatican archives
Hidden history, art
Alchemical codes
And black robed thieves
Why do we need a pandemic
Disease?

Diamond reflections
A beating heart
I am
I said
What if?
May it be
Wizard Bear said
Just watch
What happens when we
Really believe
Ya mon, said Charlie
Just watch what happens
When we really believe
Aho

The Garden is Poisoned

Eden is on fire, anyone care?

Exxon/Dow/Dupont/Monsanto
Chemicals/Pharma/Petro/Plastic
Pesticides/nuclear waste/coal

Profits before safety,
Sales before science,

89,000 new chemicals,
More everyday

Plastic choked oceans, gender blended fish

Cancers, Autism, Parkinson's, immune diseases, diabetes
The health and environment consequences
Of letting industry, Wall Street and war machine call the shots

NO ONE ACCOUNTABLE,
Never is

DUMP IT,
BURN IT,
TOSS IT,
COUNT THE MONEY...
MOVE ON.

Plastics, petro, poisons
A supercharged batshit viral killer maybe from a lab?
Endless wars
Overwhelming debt

Big Tech/Big Brother/Social Media
Apple, Facebook, Google
In your hand/in your head
On or off remote recording

Cont'd....

Privacy, freedom gone
Sold and used against you
…Now they control…
Those leftover pieces that
Used to be your mind
Is this what we want?
It's what we got

"We the People"
"Customers for Madness"

Fuck me
Fuck you
Bye bye
All
Gone

Trending Now

#Solvingthehomelessproblem
#Leadersofthepack
#Covidprevention
#Fashionforward
#Wecandothis
"Woke dogs"
Of downtown LA
Have something to say
And the little dogs
As usual had to bark
To get any attention
Chihuahuas, miniature yorkies
Weiner dogs and a couple runty bassets
And beagles
What the fuck
What the hell
Doesn't anyone notice
From down here
That trickle of
Piss
Is a goddamn yellow torrent
And those brown lumps of shit
Are mountains and pyramids
This homeless problem is getting worse every day
Millions already with us
Most here to stay
Tent cities
Urban camping
The line between us
Is dotted and thin
No insurance…
No job
One click away
Between us and them
Damaged
By wars

Cont'd…

Breakfast in Memphis: Midnight in the Desert

Bad mommy
Pedo Boy Scout camping
With those creeps in shorts, scarfs
And badges
Maybe even a priest
Or criminal injustice
Too much religion
Toxic fumes
Or just the
Luck of the draw
No healthcare
No distancing
Numbers in tent cities
Still not decreasing
Woke dogs
If you can't change humans
At least make them
Buy you shoes

Thin Dotted Line

Dawn/San Francisco
Needing caffeine…clarity even more…
Wizard Bear crossed the street for coffee…
Gave two dollars to the homeless lady sitting on the corner…
The captain of her block…
She said she'd had better days…
Maybe this would be one he thought…for both of them
The line of separation between their lives was dotted and thin…
She was up earlier than spoiled white lawyer boys…
Who imagined themselves princes and kings…
They survived on handouts too…
But sat in a more comfortable room…
Bullets for handguns…not worth the price…
Burial would save the cost of listening…
To their lies and the goddamn disgrace…
Fuck you…fuck you…fuck you…
Brooks Brothers vampires…
Never in style…
Go back to your mothers…
They already know your problems…
They dressed you badly…you never knew…
Fuck you…fuck you…fuck you…
Now go away…

Breakfast in Memphis: Midnight in the Desert

Plastic and Catholics

Celibacy is real
Doesn't work
But no exceptions

You were an alter boy
Altered a circle it's true
But enough is enough
We got bigger problems than
Even you

Neptune retained good counsel
Wants all that we have
And says it's not enough

Doesn't repair or start over
More studies not needed
Lie or evade, strike pleadings
Now proceed

Mermaids, sharks, dolphins
Whales, turtles, even little fish
All sick and dying
Just like humans
But didn't have a choice
Strange new condition
Clogging your veins
Plastic plaque build-up
Surgery not an option
Lipitor made it worse
So did birth control pills
Face creams and rest of
Big pharma

Metabolic syndrome,
Diabetes 2,
Chronic inflammation

Cont'd…

Breakfast in Memphis: Midnight in the Desert

Kidneys unable to keep up
Neptune got his lawyer

Amend the petition
Add in plastic rain

Forbidden
Fruit
Now Monsanto

Blue apples
Fish DNA
Vaccinate
Your way out
Better luck
Next time

Mind chatter

Not the time to panic

Innocent mistake

Free will really?
Not sure what happened

FDA gave approval
Patent protection granted

Upon further observations
What you see
Is what you get

Looks like more like goddamn
Junkies
Paying whatever

For one more,

Cont'd...

Breakfast in Memphis: Midnight in the Desert

Another
Just

Another

Hit

Breakfast in Memphis
There is no lunch

Snowpocalypse

Austin, TX 2021

Witch's tit
Lakes of fire
Flames of ice
Snow cones
From heaven
Popsicle dildos
Hanging from trees
Dripping
Or
Freezing
Can't make up their minds
Divine retribution
Or Hell's little treats
Welcome to Texas
Border walls
Built with
Cocaine and ice

Vegas

Color coded penguins,
Ostriches in wheelchairs,
White men wearing
Bermuda nightmares,
Gym shorts,
Stolen pajamas, slippers, sneakers,
Flip flops, short sleeve shirts and baseball caps
Diabetic women, smoking cigarettes with supersize sodas,
Pulling slots
Next time gonna be,
Las Vegas shooting no accident
This neon graveyard is where people go to die

Winners, Losers, Killers, Scoreboards

Security codes...electronic keys...a good pulse will do that
From there its easy...

Seduced by familiar language
Another losing season
It's always next time

Plantation overlord never gets better
Tax money gone for another war
Both sides, guns we always paid for
Taxpayer tab, the only one that ever pays
The bill
Vatican, Swiss, island banks and Wall Street laundromats
Open all night every day
Cleaning up those golden profits
Mafia, DEA, CIA, cartels, partnerships from hell

2020 election year
Sure
Magnetic pulses, waves of sound or light
Next year/last year always cheating
Deleted scanned altered copied
Delivered and selectively returned
This voting game is tricky
The ones allowed to vote is important

But who or what collects, and does final counting matters even more

Who best controls counting
Has the quantum power
The voter/non-voter has none
Scoreboard and clock determine winner
The counter is what you're looking for
Who sent those magnetic pulses and invisible laser beams
Tells you even more

Cont'd...

It's a cheater's world
Fools us every time
Was it foreign or domestic?
Does it matter?
Electronic money is everywhere
A blind judge is a bad symbol
It tells us too much all ready
Legal fairness is mostly fiction

Justice is blindfolded
Evidence it cannot see
No liars' faces
I swear to tell the truth
Itself another lie

When judges can't see
Or listen
And lawyers only try to win
Then justice means nothing
Weighing it like a butcher
We blindly go.
When who gets to vote
And who is counting controls elections' roulette wheel
You got a loser coming
From a game produced in hell
Odds always favor the house
When the devil is your landlord
In charge of locks and keys
You know who's keeping score

Price of Tuition

In my internal
House
At the end of a
A long winding
Hallway of deception
There is a mirror
Of flames
Melted steel
And broken glass

Plastic Jesus
Pledge of allegiance
Thoughts and prayers
Nickels, dimes, and dollars

Visa or Mastercard

All declined

Play for blood
No fear
No game

Breakfast in Memphis: Midnight in the Desert

Pledge of Allegiance

I pledge allegiance to the dollars...
Currency I can understand...
The arc of darkness surrounds me...
As I walk the valleys of my dreams...
Fear no evil...
They said they were my friends....
Nickel-plated diamonds
Can shimmer in the sun...
But when you try to cash them in...
You're done...

Pelvic Roulette

Pelvic roulette
The oldest new game in town
Casino royale
To win you gotta play
To play you got to win

Heavenly Chess

Breakfast in London
Mortal knights and bishops
Paid tribute to the death of
The queen
An infinite board
Millions of pawns
Moving forward one
Step at a time
Captured too easy
Stuck in the past
Frozen by rules
Guarding the king
Protecting the queen
Do we need a new board
And some upgraded pieces?

Signals of the Blind

Institutional blindness is an acquired habit
Situational blindness/temporary insanity

Criminally insane or just a little evil

Sounds like a Vanderbilt problem

True love meets lonely at the dog pound
Trust the plan

From the Q-puff?
On the down low

Don't shoot the messenger
You didn't hear it from me

Wrong map, scenic route, road construction

Road sign confusion
Slippery when wet

Green light?
Yellow light?
Or flashing red?

Halfway to Barstow
Last exit was Hell
Nevada Testing Grounds/Area 51
Burning Man, Reno, and Vegas

Desert rain/nuclear rainbows
Let's meet under
God's umbrella
I'll bring the sunshine
You bring the rain

Blame It on the Full Moon

Blame it on the full moon
Mercury left retrograde

Know what I mean?
Heard what you said!

Sex and life in the QAnon age
Excuses are dangerous
Responsibility = a tax for living
Duty-free is an airport store
Mixed signals
A prep school defense
Missed signals
Inattention to detail
Failure to breath
Can be fatal

Green looks like red
Colorblind workers
In a paint store
All sales final

Everyday Confusion

It's a quarter to five
What day is it really
I haven't a clue
Maybe if you tell me
I would know what to do
Sweet Jesus I doubt it
You pitiful fool
How do I know?
I share the same doorway
Blind and confused
Looking for colors
Unable to move

Who Knows?

Who knows the secrets
To why it's all going down
Lots of them claim they know
Most are lying or deceived

Truth in an Alley

Truth in an alley
Dim lights
Soft lies
Negotiating
The price
Is only half the battle

Indoor Rain

Indoor rain...
Keeps falling...
Toxic legacy...
Truth and justice...
Replaced by greed...
A curse bought...
With cash…
In the name of God...
Spells the end…
For humanity...
"Exxon Mobil"
New odds 40-1

Buffalo Hunter

Punishment and relief
Deprived, lost, or hungry
A crumb of bread or recognition
Means everything
The board changes
But the game is the same.
Find the fat, rich, scared, and sloppy…
Like buffalo on the prairie
Feed the village for a week
We've been looking at those buffalo
And the hunters for awhile now,
The hunters got guns
And the buffalo got hungry
More hunters now
Gotta make more buffalo
Sooner or later gonna
Look in the mirror
Am I the fat beast
Or one of the hunters

Misdemeanor Monday

It was a misdemeanor Monday...
But the judge was still keeping score...
The sobriety pills weren't working...
Whiskey bottles on the floor...
Guess we need to double the dose...
So you can understand...
Bailiff take the man away...
It's time for another hand...
The game goes on...and on
Round the clock...
The players go in and out...
Politicians stack the deck...
Paid for by the state...
Prosecutors take their pick...
It doesn't really matter...
The players just rotate...
Metal detectors and sheriffs pat you down...
Can't take knives to a gunfight...
Wouldn't help much anyway...
The weapons of mass destruction are waiting just inside
Cause the game goes on and on...

Full Metal Mueller

Driving to Los Angeles
Summer 1947
Cross long dry fields
Of fallen ships
Ruinous make-believe
The truth was buried
Deep inside
Planetary angels
Mormons, masons
Vatican thieves
Flashing Nazi symbols
Paperclip devils
CIA, CIA
Devils got the DNA
Variants left
Variants right
Variants down the middle
Solve this first
Solve this last
Lost in endless riddles

Low Frequency Shoes

Those low frequency shoes
Are bringing me down
Killing the buzz
Tapping my soul
Twitching my bones
And nerves
Ruining my sleep
The jackhammer in the sky
Is not helping
Internet, Twitter, and Facebook
Three final nails in our coffin

Kool-Aid and TV

Blame it on the devil
Living on Kool-Aid
And watching TV
Got you confused
What preacher to believe
Now you got trouble
Like never before
Sympathy for the devil
Just not my cup of tea

Matrix

Alive in the matrix
Dead in the streets
Channeling disease
Lies and confusion
Or is it just TV

Breakfast in Memphis: Midnight in the Desert

Faded Ink

I don't need your expectations
I got plenty of my own
Black dawns and endless
Nights
Numbered lists
Of wished for dreams
All too often dried up
And dated
Expired, forgotten, failed
Or lost
Buried without a funeral
Faded ink on
Paper headstones
White or yellow
Many never read again

Quarter Past Three

Wizard Bear noticed
It was quarter past three
The lights in his head were
Barely lit and
Flickering dim
Charlie the Dragon
Had long packed it in
The endless downtown
Party fueled
By booze, drugs, and hormones
Had attracted parasites
Energy sucking entities
Like mosquitos or leeches
Some stayed attached
Invisible riders
Hitching and hiding
Fueled on drama, sugar
Alcohol, pain, and cocaine
Stop feeding the vampires
A little evil is still evil
And there is no room
In your world and nothing to gain
Addicted to
Weakness
Distraction
Self-delusion
Confusion
Chaos
And blame

Breakfast in Memphis: Midnight in the Desert

Eternal Fools

Eternal fools
On circus rides
Looking back
At our own reflections
The days go by uncounted
Hidden right below
The very best intentions

Breakfast in Memphis: Midnight in the Desert

Bad Day in the Mirror

Burn it
Leave it
Give it up
Yes you
That stay puff
Liar in the mirror

Flush it
Bleed it
Freeze it
Burn it
Not even
Your own mother
Still believes it
Warm Southern winds

Just too
Easy

Breakfast in Memphis: Midnight in the Desert

Coffee and Tears

The wounds you can't see
It was a different kind
Of injury
Happens everywhere
In many ways
And for many reasons
Or none at all
Invisible blood
Silent wounds
But it was there

Lost in the Woods

Terror in the forest
When you realize
The trees are not your friends
And they cover up the sunshine
And you can't find your way home

Breakfast in Memphis: Midnight in the Desert

Blind Men and Broken Mirrors

In a world beyond delusion
Perhaps there is a plan
Until then it's guessing games
And riddles
Distraction is still distraction
Medication doubles down
Silent pain keeps growing
Hidden in hearts and bones

Breakfast in Memphis: Midnight in the Desert

One Blade of Grass

It's what I remember
Of life...
The torn shattered pieces
Over chewed...
Undigested
Impossible to swallow
Sometimes just thrown up
A blinking neon arrow
Reminds me.
Take it easy
One blade of grass
Is all you'll ever know

Stolen Spring

Broken glass and shattered
Dreams left pieces of my reflection
Laying on the ground
Cut my feet
With memories I can't
Quite see
Blood dripping
Silently
White carpet words
With scarlet ink
Blurred by life
Painful to recall

Too Dark to Notice

Some days it's just too dark
To notice
Our own internal
Suns,
Blinded by reflected
Light
Coming in from all
Directions

Exodus

Did I stay too long
To notice
That I was no longer here
Exodus relieved the pain
Of dying
And endless frozen tears

Mud and Madness

Sludging through the
Mud of our daily
Existence
Seeking relief
From self-inflicted
Pain and madness
What is the key
To reason and hope
Is that where we go
For humor and light
Or do we tumble and fall
In decay
And perpetual depression?

Dangling

Looking for reassurance
In the smallest of things
To relieve the terror
And uncertainty
Of human beings
Always dangling
By a thin
Imaginary
String

Tethered
To whatever
Nothing in between

Breakfast in Memphis: Midnight in the Desert

Being Human

Being human
Is a fatal disease
Time is limited
By unknown factors
At least this time around
If that's what you believe
Some seem so convincing
About reincarnation
Other dimensions
Angels and helpers
And cosmic realities
I wish I knew what to believe
Meanwhile down here
On earth,
In my city,
My house,
My body,
I ask simple
Questions
Who am I?
What do I want?
What do I do?

Speed Limits/Fools

Everything I know about myself and everyone else is wrong...
The cook in the back burning bacon and wondering why...
Knows more about your life than you do...
The white line down the middle went straight to your brain...
The speed limit was 75...
There was no limit on fools...

North Side of Town

The positive
Side of Covid
Is hanging out
On the north side of town
Slow down
Open wide
Get ready for the changing
A new kind of tide
Water tiger
Pluto and Neptune
Shifting degrees
Falling backwards
Without gravity
And time
Makes for some
Interesting results
Is that so?
Ya mon
See you Tuesday
On the north side of town
"Ya mon"

Chemical Judy: A Modern Polymer Romance

DuPont was her daddy
Her sister is poly
The brother is Trey or Trip
Rich people, why is that
Branding starts early?
Or bad memory for names

Cute Vanderbilt nicknames
For southern frat fucks
From family money
Rich make you stupid?

And first born boy always
Named after daddy

Long as he's not black
These DuPont girls were popular
Even more than expected

Love at first sight
She was cheap,
She was easy
Love it, leave it
Dump it when done

Daddy don't mind
He's too busy making more

Night Bank

Opens after dark
Closes at dawn
7 days a week
Borrowing from the night
For those times
When daytime is just
Not enough
No credit check
If you can stay up
You can borrow
Payment plans
Negotiated with
Your body
I was a special favored customer
At night bank
For decades
Night after night
Week after week

Month after month
Year after year

There was the time
I hosted the let's stay up
The rest of our lives party
In Houston after law school
And invited several friends
To test the idea that
Sleep is a psychological
Not biological need
We can get so much more done
Without sleep I thought
I made it longer than anyone else
8 days
Interesting times
Until

The Valley of Oppression

The valley of oppression was
Long, deep and filled with cactus
Snakes and demons
Hid in plain view
The sun was hot
Too hot
And it was windy
So windy
The path was uneven
And rocky
So rocky
The journey was long
So long
Progress was slow
So slow
The trek was unending
And this was just day one
The sun went down
The moon came up
The temperature dropped
And now is cold
Too cold
And still windy
Too windy
This was still day one
The sun came up
And there it was
The mountain

It was a big mountain
The closer we got
The bigger it was
Too big
Impossibly big
One step at a time
We can do it
Oh hell no, it's too
Big and scary
We should just stop
Now before we go
Any further
So we did
And quit
Without climbing the mountain
It was too high, too hot
Too cold, and too windy
We shouldn't even have tried
So the group turned around
And retreated
Arriving home lost
And defeated
It was too hot, too cold
Too windy, too big
The fear was justified
The people were tired
It was so hot, so cold
So windy, the path
Was so narrow and rocky
And then the mountain cried

Breakfast in Memphis: Midnight in the Desert

Midnight in the Desert

Do humans enjoy killing
Raping
Lying
And stealing?
Is it done out of believed necessity
Revenge
Or justification
Do we believe it doesn't matter
Or because we just don't care
I am afraid the answer is all of the
Above and more
It is midnight in the desert
There may not be much more

Questions and Answers

Prayers for clarity
And power

Visionary fool
Went wandering
Down by the lake
What had become of
Magic he created years ago
Certain it seemed

Yet never took place
Time tables broken
Overlooked obstacles
So many mistakes
Overconfidence
Improper planning

Too many distractions
Or wrong time and place
Midnight in the desert
Coming up soon
Will portals of power
And hidden dimensions
Be answering soon
Climbing dark mountains
Well before dawn
Greeting the sunrise
On top of the peak
What did we learn
Where do we go next
Aho

Breakfast in Memphis: Midnight in the Desert

17 Guns

17 guns
17 soldiers
Which one
Is gonna die?
Another day
In the battlefield
Which one
Is gonna die?
Can we agree
This is madness
Which one
Is gonna die?
17 guns
17 soldiers
Which one
Is gonna die?
16 guns
16 soldiers
A mother somewhere
Is crying
Which one is
Next to die
Can we agree
This is madness
Which one
Is gonna die
15 guns
15 solders
A mother
And father
Somewhere
Are crying
Which one
Is gonna
Die next
Can we agree

Cont'd…

This is madness
Too many soldiers
Have died
Ya mon
Too many soldiers
Have died
Can we just agree
This is madness
Too many soldiers
Have died
Ya mon
Too many soldiers
Have died
This is just madness
Too many soldiers
Have died
14 guns
14 soldiers
Sisters and brothers
Are crying
Their Marine corps
Brother is
Not
Coming
Home
Can we finally
Agree this is madness
And bring our boys
And girls home
Ya mon
Just bring our boys
And girls home
Can't we see
This is madness
Just bring them
All home
Ya mon
Just bring them all home

Cont'd…

Breakfast in Memphis: Midnight in the Desert

This is madness
Just put down the weapons
And bring them all home

White Collar Criminals

While I lay sleeping, the voices came to me,
They told the story of wickedness and injustice
They told me doctors and lawyers were the criminal ones
They said this was nothing compared to all that has been done
In the name of royal professions and the companies they kept
They hurt the women
They hurt the men
It makes no difference to them
Not now, not then
It's punishment for witchcraft
Standing up, or being born
Makes no difference to them
Not now, not then
Been this way a thousand years
It'll be a thousand more
You see, people make it easy
For the liars and thieves to seem real
It's just too hard for us to think they really steal
Cause they went to all the best schools
They live in fine clean houses and work in shiny buildings of glass and steel
Would they pay a federal judge to look the other way?
Oh no, no…cause after all they went to all the finest schools
They live in fine clean houses, they work in shiny buildings of glass and steel
It can't be real

ABOUT THE AUTHOR

Breakfast in Memphis Vol. 2: Midnight in the Desert is the second in a series of poetry by Austin, Texas and Atlanta, Georgia trial lawyer, Mark Mueller. "Several years ago, these words just came into my head, unpredictably, late at night, early in the morning, while walking in downtown cities, in times of isolation, pain, loss, disappointment, crisis, love, regret, awe and joy. They often seemed to almost type themselves onto my cell phone or iPad, usually perfectly formed and complete, sometimes in pairs or bunches, and slowly they accumulated into Breakfast in Memphis."

Mark Mueller is recognized for his work in birth injury litigation and product liability cases involving damages from unsafe medical devices, chemicals and pharmaceuticals. His work has twice led to FDA safety advisories for both vacuum extractors and vaginal mesh, and then eventual removal of many dangerous transvaginal mesh devices from the market.

He successfully represented the Brave Dog Society of the Blackfoot tribe in preventing oil and gas development in a pristine national wilderness area of Montana. Mark is also counsel for the Lakota

Cont'd...

Sioux Sundance Chiefs regarding ownership rights to sacred ceremonial objects.

A number of his precedent setting, high profile cases have been featured in the national media including, most notably, Oprah, Good Morning America, Special Insider Edition, The New York Times, Texas Lawyer and National Law Journal.

Mark's production company, Voodoo Cowboy Entertainment, hosted annual musical and art performance parties for many years. Through his production company, he also served as associate/executive producer for independent films including *Downloading Nancy* (Sundance Festival), *Winter in the Blood, Slam Planet, The Two Bob's,* and Ed Brown's environmental documentary *A New Resistance.* He was a featured speaker and panelist for Conscious Media Festival programs on topics of sustainability and creating positive culture change.

Mark is currently developing a comprehensive and innovative legal strategy and support network called the Truth and Justice League. The goal of the Truth and Justice League is to address the nation's disastrous environmentally toxic legacy in ways that will hold wrongdoers accountable and lay the foundation for a more sustainable future. The hope is to restore personal freedom and democracy through active citizen involvement, jury trials, and a more informed and participatory voting public.

Mark is also the author of Unicorn Park, a children's poetry book, Breakfast in Memphis Vol. 1: Universe Favors the Hero and Breakfast in Memphis Vol. 3: Colors of Love.

ABOUT THE ARTIST

Cover Art by Analy Nakat
Instagram: @analynakat
www.analynakat.com

Analy Nakat is a full-time artist living in Los Angeles, CA working in various mediums including painting, drawing, collaborative projects, tattoos, and music. A native of Lebanon, her family fled war and relocated to the state of Texas when she was 13, where she struggled to assimilate into American culture. At the age of 18, Analy left Texas and moved to the San Francisco Bay Area, where she studied illustration at the California College of the Arts

Her haunting, often surreal work is revealed through a magical world that incorporates images of women, animals, plants and the patterns of nature, all of it suffused with a fascination with anthropology.

"Seeing how diverse people can live, and how people can adapt, I try to create magical places where people live in harmony with nature on canvas."

Breakfast in Memphis: Midnight in the Desert

Find other volumes in the Breakfast in Memphis series here:

https://www.truthandjusticeleague.com/books

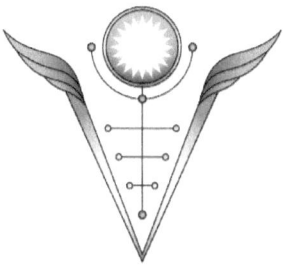

www.ingramcontent.com/pod-product-compliance
Lightning Source LLC
Chambersburg PA
CBHW050856150626
46549CB00013B/2411